PRE-APPRENTICESHIP
MATHS & LITERACY FOR
BRICKLAYING

Graduated exercises and practice exam

Andrew Spencer

A+ National Pre-apprenticeship Maths & Literacy for Bricklaying
1st Edition
Andrew Spencer

Publishing editor: Sarah Broomhall
Project editor: Aynslie Harper
Proofreader: Katharine Day
Text designer: Miranda Costa
Cover designer: Aisling Gallagher
Cover image: Shutterstock.com/hxdbzxy
Permissions researcher: Wendy Duncan
Production controller: Emma Roberts
Typeset by: Q2A Media

Any URLs contained in this publication were checked for currency during the production process. Note, however, that the publisher cannot vouch for the ongoing currency of URLs.

© 2016 Cengage Learning Australia Pty Limited

For product information and technology assistance,
in Australia call **1300 790 853**;
in New Zealand call **0800 449 725**

For permission to use material from this text or product, please email
aust.permissions@cengage.com

ISBN 978 0 17 047388 0

Cengage Learning Australia
Level 7, 80 Dorcas Street
South Melbourne, Victoria Australia 3205

Cengage Learning New Zealand
Unit 4B Rosedale Office Park
331 Rosedale Road, Albany, North Shore 0632, NZ

For learning solutions, visit **cengage.com.au**

Printed in Australia by Ligare Pty Limited.
1 2 3 4 5 6 7 26 25 24 23 22

A+ National
PRE-APPRENTICESHIP
Maths & Literacy for Bricklaying

Contents

Introduction

It has always been important to understand, from a teacher's perspective, the nature of the mathematical skills students need for their future, rather than teaching them 'textbook mathematics'. This has been a guiding principle behind the development of the content in this workbook. To teach maths that is *relevant* to students seeking apprenticeships is the best that we can do, to give students an education in the field that they would like to work in.

The content in this resource is aimed at the level that is needed for students to have the best possibility of improving their maths and literacy skills specifically for trades. Students can use this workbook to prepare for an apprenticeship entry assessment, or to even assist with basic numeracy and literacy at the VET/TAFE level. Coupled with the NelsonNet website, https://www.nelsonnet.com.au/free-resources, these resources have the potential to improve the students' understanding of basic mathematical concepts that can be applied to trades. These resources have been trialled, and they work.

Commonly used trade terms are introduced so that students have a basic understanding of terminology that they will encounter in the workplace environment. Students who can complete this workbook and reach an 80 per cent or higher outcome in all topics will have achieved the goal of this resource. These students will go on to complete work experience, do a VET accredited course, or will be able to gain entry into VET/TAFE or an apprenticeship in the trade of their choice.

The content in this workbook is the first step to bridging the gap between what has been learnt in previous years, and what needs to be remembered and re-learnt for use in trades. Students will significantly benefit from the consolidation of the basic maths and literacy concepts.

Every school has students who want to work with their hands, and not all students want to go to university. The best students want to learn what they don't already know; and if students want to learn, then this book has the potential to give them a good start in life.

This resource has been specifically tailored to prepare students for sitting apprenticeship or VET/TAFE admission tests, and for giving students the basic skills they will need for a career in trade. In many ways, it is a win–win situation, with students enjoying and studying relevant maths for work, and Trades and Registered Training Officers (RTOs) receiving students who have improved basic maths and literacy skills.

All that is needed from students is patience, hard work, a positive attitude, a belief in themselves that they can do it and a desire to achieve.

About the author

Andrew graduated from SACAE Underdale in 1988 with a Bachelor of Education. In 1989, Andrew went on to attend West Virginia University, where he completed a Master of Science (specialising in teacher education), while lecturing part-time.

In 1993, Andrew moved to NSW and began teaching at Sydney Boys' High, where he taught in a range of subject areas including Mathematics, English, Science, Classics, Physical Education and Technical Studies. His sense of practical mathematics continued to develop with the range of subject areas he taught in.

Andrew moved back to South Australia in 1997 with a diverse knowledge base and an understanding of the importance of using mathematics in different practical subject areas. He began teaching with the De La Salle Brothers in 1997 in South Australia, where he continues to work and teach today. Andrew has worked in collaboration with the SACE Board to help develop resources for mathematics with a practical focus.

In 2011, Andrew was awarded the John Gaffney Mathematics Education Trust Award for valuable contributions to the teaching of Mathematics in South Australia. Andrew received a Recognition of Excellence for outstanding contributions to the teaching profession by CEASA in both 2011 and 2012 and, in 2014, he was one of 12 teachers from across Australia to work in collaboration with the Chief Scientist of Australia to develop a better understanding of the role of mathematics in industry. As part of this role, he undertook research in this area, spent time working with the industry and then fed the results back to the Chief Scientist.

Andrew continues to develop the pre-apprenticeship and vocational titles, based on mathematics and literacy, to assist and support the learning of students who want to follow a vocational career path. He is currently working towards the nineteenth title in this series. The titles have also been adapted in the UK and Asia, as the importance of this type of functional mathematics continues to grow. All schools have students who will follow a vocational pathway and it continues to be a strong focus of Andrew's to support the learning needs of these students.

Acknowledgements

For Paula, Zach, Katelyn, Mum and Dad.

To the De La Salle Brothers for their selfless work with all students.

To Dr Pauline Carter for her unwavering support of all Mathematics teachers.

To all students who value learning, who are willing to work hard and who have character … and are characters!

LITERACY

Unit 1: Spelling

Short-answer questions

Specific instructions to students

- This is an exercise to help you to identify and correct spelling errors.
- Read the activity below and then answer accordingly.

Read the following passage, and identify and correct the spelling errors.

Jack arrived on site early because his boss had mensioned the importanse of an apprentice getting trowel experience early on in an aprenticeship. Jack also knew that his boss ekpected him to 'pay his way' in terms of bricks laid each day, so he desided to start earliar than usual to show his boss that he is keen to work.

Generaly, bricklayers get paid for the volume of bricks that they lay. The average rate is between 300 to 500 bricks per day, depending on the whether. A bricklayer is also requred to do other daily tasks, such as mix and spread mortar, seal foundations and use verious tools to cut and shape bricks.

Jack's boss told him that earning rates fluctuete in the construction industry, acording to building demend. Estimates for the cost of a job can be caluclated based on how many briks an apprentice bricklayer needs to lay, in order to 'pay their way'. This is compared to the hourly aprentice costs, which can include travel alowances, insuranse, off-site trainning costs, downtime and insentives.

Incorrect words:

_____

_____

Correct words:

_____

_____

Unit 2: Alphabetising

Short-answer questions

Specific instructions to students

- In this unit, you will be able to practise your alphabetising skills.
- Read the activity below and then answer accordingly.

Put the following words into alphabetical order.

Trowel	Mortar
Safety boots	Overalls
Block	Cement
Building plan	Hammer
Hammer drill	Brick
Drawings	Brick saw
Chalk line	Safety glasses

Answer:

_____

_____

_____

_____

_____

_____

_____

_____

_____

_____

_____

_____

_____

_____

age fotostock/german-images

Short-answer questions

Specific instructions to students

- This is an exercise to help you understand what you read.
- Read the following activity and then answer the questions that follow.

Read the following passage and answer the questions in full sentences.

Josh is interested in becoming a bricklayer because his Dad was a bricklayer. He decides to ask a family friend, Chris, who also works as a 'bricklayer', what the trade is like. 'So, what does a bricklayer do?' Josh asks. Chris replies, 'A bricklayer prepares and lays bricks, stone, structure tiles, marble, concrete blocks and any other masonry materials to build or repair walls, partitions, fireplaces, sewers or other structures. A bricklayer does plenty of different jobs'.

'What about skills and attributes?' asks Josh.

'A bricklayer needs certain skills and attributes', replies Chris, 'such as manual dexterity, a good sense of balance, strength and stamina to work with heavy tools and materials, the ability to work at heights, strength to move heavy ladders and to know how to set up scaffolding as well'.

Josh enquired further. 'What are the working conditions like?'

'Bricklayers normally work a five-day, 38-hour week when possible; however, overtime is often required to meet construction schedules. Some self-employed bricklayers will work longer hours, including weekends, to complete the job. Work is mainly outdoors and we often have to climb on scaffolding. The work is physically demanding most of the time. You need to get and keep your driver's licence, too, so that you can get to and from the work sites', said Chris. 'That's heaps!' Josh exclaims.

'Is that it or is there be anything else that I'd need to do?' Josh asks.

'Well, bricklayers may need to perform some other tasks too, such as working from plans, sealing foundations with damp-resistant materials, building door and window frames, checking vertical and horizontal alignment of bricks and blocks, using tools and brick-cutting machines to cut and shape bricks, building arches and ornamental brickwork, repairing and maintaining clay bricks, and safely erect scaffolding', responds Chris.

QUESTION 1

Why does Josh want to become a bricklayer?

Answer:

_____

QUESTION 2

What are the 'different jobs' that a bricklayer may need to do?

Answer:

_____

_____

QUESTION 3

What physical attributes should a bricklayer have?

Answer:

_____

_____

_____

QUESTION 4

What are the working conditions that a bricklayer may encounter?

Answer:

_____

_____

_____

_____

Alamy/Image Source Plus

QUESTION 5

Why is it important for an apprentice to get and keep a driver's licence?

Answer:

_____

MATHEMATICS

Unit 4: General Mathematics

Short-answer questions

Specific instructions to students

- This unit is designed to help you to improve your general mathematical skills.
- Read the following questions and answer all of them in the spaces provided.
- You may not use a calculator.
- You need to show all working.

QUESTION 1

What unit of measurement is used to measure:

a   the length of a brick?

Answer:

_____

b   the pressure produced by a compressor?

Answer:

_____

c   the amount of mortar needed for a job?

Answer:

_____

d   the weight of a ready-mix cement bag?

Answer:

_____

e   the speed of a vehicle?

Answer:

_____

f   the length of a chalk line?

Answer:

_____

g   the cost of a hammer?

Answer:

_____

QUESTION 2

Give examples of how the following might be used in the bricklaying industry.

a   percentages

Answer:

_____

b   decimals

Answer:

_____

c   fractions

Answer:

_____

d   mixed numbers

Answer:

_____

e   ratios

Answer:

_____

f   angles

Answer:

_____

QUESTION 3

Convert the following units.

a   1.2 metres to cm and mm

Answer:

_____

b   4 tonne to kg

Answer:

_____

c   260 centimetres to mm

Answer:

_____

d   1140 mL to litres

Answer:

_____

e   1650 g to kilograms

Answer:

_____

f   1.8 kg to grams

Answer:

_____

g   3 metres to cm and mm

Answer:

_____

h   4.5 L to millilitres

Answer:

_____

QUESTION 4

Write the following in descending order.

0.4   0.04   4.1   40.0   400.00   4.0

Answer:

_____

QUESTION 5

Write the decimal number that is between:

a   0.2 and 0.4

Answer:

_____

b   1.8 and 1.9

Answer:

_____

c   12.4 and 12.5

Answer:

_____

d   28.3 and 28.4

Answer:

_____

e   101.5 and 101.7

Answer:

_____

QUESTION 6

Round off the following numbers to two (2) decimal places.

a   12.346

Answer:

_____

b   2.251

Answer:

_____

c   123.897

Answer:

_____

d   688.882

Answer:

_____

e   1209.741

Answer:

_____

9780170473880

QUESTION 7

Estimate the following by approximation.

a $1288 \times 19 =$

Answer:

_____

b $201 \times 20 =$

Answer:

_____

c $497 \times 12.2 =$

Answer:

_____

d $1008 \times 10.3 =$

Answer:

_____

e $399 \times 22 =$

Answer:

_____

f $201 - 19 =$

Answer:

_____

g $502 - 61 =$

Answer:

_____

h $1003 - 49 =$

Answer:

_____

i $10\,001 - 199 =$

Answer:

_____

j $99.99 - 39.8 =$

Answer:

_____

QUESTION 8

What do the following add up to?

a $4, $4.99 and $144.95

Answer:

_____

b   8.75, 6.9 and 12.55

Answer:

_____

c   650 mm, 1800 mm and 2290 mm

Answer:

_____

d   21.3 mm, 119.8 mm and 884.6 mm

Answer:

_____

QUESTION 9

Subtract the following.

a   2338 from 7117

Answer:

_____

b   1786 from 3112

Answer:

_____

c   5979 from 8014

Answer:

_____

d   11 989 from 26 221

Answer:

_____

e   108 767 from 231 111

Answer:

_____

QUESTION 10

Use division to solve the following.

a $2177 \div 7 =$

Answer:

b $4484 \div 4 =$

Answer:

c $63.9 \div 0.3 =$

Answer:

d $121.63 \div 1.2 =$

Answer:

e $466.88 \div 0.8$

Answer:

The following information is provided for question 11.

To solve using BODMAS, in order from left to right, solve the **B**rackets first, then **O**f, then **D**ivision, then **M**ultiplication, then **A**ddition and lastly **S**ubtraction. The following example has been done for your reference.

EXAMPLE

Solve $(4 \times 7) \times 2 + 6 - 4$.

STEP 1

Solve the Brackets first: $(4 \times 7) = 28$.

STEP 2

No Division so next solve Multiplication: $28 \times 2 = 56$.

STEP 3

Addition is next: $56 + 6 = 62$.

STEP 4

Subtraction is the last process: $62 - 4 = 58$.

FINAL ANSWER:

58

QUESTION 11

Use BODMAS to solve the following.

a $(6 \times 9) \times 5 + 7 - 2 =$

Answer:

b $(9 \times 8) \times 4 + 6 - 1 =$

Answer:

c $3 \times (5 \times 7) + 11 - 8 =$

Answer:

d $6 + 9 - 5 \times (8 \times 3) =$

Answer:

e $9 - 7 + 6 \times 3 + (9 \times 6) =$

Answer:

f $6 + 9 \times 4 + (6 \times 7) - 21 =$

Answer:

amana images/Ian Lishman

Section A: Addition

QUESTION 1

Shutterstock.com/valda

A bricklayer uses a string line to check the lengths of a wall and to make sure the wall is straight. The walls measure 2 m, 1 m, 3 m and 5 m. How much length has been measured in total?

Answer:

QUESTION 2

Four lengths of brick wall measure 5 m, 8 m, 13 m and 15 m. How much brick wall length is there in total?

Answer:

QUESTION 3

A warehouse stocks 2170 of the '100 × 3.0 × 15 mm' cut-off disks, 368 of the '105 × 1.0 × 16 mm' cut-off disks and 723 various other cut-off disks. How many cut-off disks are in stock?

Answer:

QUESTION 4

An apprentice bricklayer travels 282 km in the first week, 344 km in the second week, 489 km in the third week and 111 km in the fourth week. How many kilometres have been driven over the four weeks?

Answer:

QUESTION 5

A bricklaying company uses the following number of inject mortar tubes at different worksites: 32 in the first week, 47 in the second week, 57 in the third week and 59 in the fourth week. How many tubes have been used in total?

Answer:

QUESTION 6

A bricklayer buys a utility brush for $22, four brick line holders for $16 and two pairs of gloves for $9. How much has the bricklayer spent?

Answer:

QUESTION 7

A national bricklaying company buys 86 300-mm dummy clamps, 132 180-mm dummy clamps and 97 550-mm dummy clamps. How many dummy clamps have been purchased?

Answer:

QUESTION 8

A bricklayer buys a 14-inch brick saw, which has a 1700W electric motor and a stand and mitre guide, for $1589, three 1.5-m clamped handle screeds for $169 and two 1200-mm levels for $209. How much money has been spent?

Answer:

QUESTION 9

The lengths of the new brick walls that need to be constructed for a retirement village are 16 m for one wall, 18 m for another wall, 8 m for another wall and 11 m for the last wall. How many metres of wall need to be built in total?

Answer:

QUESTION 10

A bricklayer uses 178 kg of mortar on one job, 188 kg on another and 93 kg on a third job. How many kilograms are used in total?

Answer:

Section B: Subtraction

Short-answer questions

Specific instructions to students

- This section is designed to help you to improve your subtraction skills for basic operations.
- Read the questions below and answer all of them in the spaces provided.
- You may not use a calculator.
- You need to show all working.

QUESTION 1

An apprentice's car is filled with petrol to its limit of 52 litres on payday. If 12 litres are used on Friday, 13 litres used on Saturday and 11 litres used on Sunday, how much petrol remains in the tank for work on Monday?

Answer:

QUESTION 2

Over a week, bags of mortar weighing a total of 500 kg are delivered to different worksites. If 250 kg are delivered first, then a further 125 kg, how many kilograms remain to be delivered?

Answer:

QUESTION 3

If Richard lays 243 concrete bricks on one job and Jamie lays 159 concrete bricks on another job, how many more bricks has Richard laid than Jamie?

Answer:

QUESTION 4

If an apprentice lays 12 concrete blocks from a pallet that has 90 concrete blocks on it, how many are left?

Answer:

QUESTION 5

A top-of-the-range steel wheelbarrow with square corners is advertised for $230. The manager offers a discount of $27. How much does the customer pay?

Answer:

QUESTION 6

A site manager orders 5000 concrete blocks. Bricklayers use 2756 blocks over a few weeks. How many blocks remain?

Answer:

QUESTION 7

An area on a building plan totals $96\,m^2$. If $44\,m^2$ is used to store general equipment and $17\,m^2$ is used to store tools, how much space, in square metres, is left?

Answer:

QUESTION 8

iStockphoto/Wicki58

A bricklayer uses 69 230-mm diamond blades over a set period. If there were a total of 105 diamond blades to begin with, how many remain?

Answer:

QUESTION 9

The odometer of a work van has a reading of 56 089 km at the start of the year. At the end of the year, it reads 71 101 km. How many kilometres have been travelled during the year?

Answer:

QUESTION 10

A construction worker uses 31 bricks on one window, 29 on another window and 103 bricks on another window. If there were 250 bricks to begin with, how many are now left?

Answer:

Section C: Multiplication

Short-answer questions

Specific instructions to students

- This section is designed to help you to improve your multiplication skills for basic operations.
- Read the following questions and answer all of them in the spaces provided.
- You may not use a calculator.
- You need to show all working.

QUESTION 1

A bricklayer charges $40 per hour. How much is earned for a 45-hour week?

Answer:

QUESTION 2

If an apprentice has 14 105-mm diamond blades in one box, how many are in 15 boxes?

Answer:

QUESTION 3

A van uses 13 litres of diesel for one trip to a worksite. How much fuel is used if the van makes the same trip each day for 18 days?

Answer:

QUESTION 4

Throughout the day, a bricklayer uses 48 metres of polyproof on a job. How many metres are needed if the bricklayer completed the same job 24 times?

Answer:

QUESTION 5

An apprentice bricklayer uses 330 bricks to build a 6-metre wall at a housing estate. Six more walls of the same dimensions need to be built. How many bricks are needed?

Answer:

QUESTION 6

A bricklayer uses 16 kg of cement to finish off the top of a foundation. How many kilograms are needed for 15 of the same job?

Answer:

QUESTION 7

A labourer's car uses 9 litres of LPG every 100 km. How much LPG is used for 450 km?

Answer:

QUESTION 8

If 673 bags of render are used per month by a major company, how many bags are used over a year?

Answer:

QUESTION 9

If a worker uses eight tubes of inject mortar each day, how many are used during a 31-day month?

Answer:

QUESTION 10

If a car travelling to a country worksite travels at 110 km/h for five hours, how far has it travelled?

Answer:

Section D: Division

Short-answer questions

Specific instructions to students

- This section is designed to help you to improve your division skills for basic operations.
- Read the questions below and answer all of them in the spaces provided.
- You may not use a calculator.
- You need to show all working.

QUESTION 1

A labourer works a total of 24 hours over three days. How many hours are worked each day?

Answer:

QUESTION 2

An experienced bricklayer earns $868 for working a five-day week. How much is earned per day?

Answer:

QUESTION 3

iStockphoto/johnnyscriv

To finish off some brickwork, 140 bricks are needed on four corners of a building. How many bricks are used on each corner? Are there any bricks left over?

Answer:

QUESTION 4

A delivery truck carrying concrete blocks covers 780 km in a five-day week. On average, how many kilometres per day have been travelled?

Answer:

QUESTION 5

Eighty-eight bricks are required to finish off around four windows. How many bricks are allocated evenly to each window?

Answer:

QUESTION 6

A bricklayer uses 2926 blocks on seven different jobs. On average, how many blocks are used for each job?

Answer:

QUESTION 7

A worker at a brickmaking company counts 2326 blocks that have already been made. If the blocks are stocked in 100 lots, how many lots are there? Are there any blocks left over?

Answer:

QUESTION 8

A manager orders 408 bags of 20-kg cement to be used for a job on a building site. If the bags are put in six-bag lots, how many lots are there?

Answer:

QUESTION 9

A bricklayer uses 450 bricks on three separate jobs on a worksite. How many bricks are allocated to each of the three jobs if the same number are needed for each job?

Answer:

amana images/Ian Lishman

QUESTION 10

A building inspector travels 3890 km in 28 days, inspecting worksites. On average, how many kilometres are travelled each day?

Answer:

Section A: Addition

QUESTION 1

If an apprentice buys four sets of screwdrivers for a total of $137.99 and a claw hammer for $22.70, how much is spent in total?

Answer:

QUESTION 2

A contractor purchases a drill for $39.95, a set of drill bits for $29.95, a trowel for $44.55 and a set of clamps for $19.45. How much money is spent?

Answer:

QUESTION 3

A 7-inch gauging trowel with a soft grip costs $29.85, a quick-action 200-mm sliding clamp costs $19.50 and a 25-mm top clamp (internal G bracket only) costs $15.65. What is the total cost?

Answer:

QUESTION 4

The height of one scaffold platform measures 1105.5 mm and the height of another measures 988.5 mm. What is the total height of the scaffold platforms if they are placed on top of each other?

Answer:

QUESTION 5

An apprentice buys the following items for work: a grooved plugging chisel for $8.99, a set of steel raker wheels and rivets for $6.50, a #8 50-m lime stringline for $6.50 and a 4.5-inch heavy-duty bolster with wrist guard for $25.99. What is the total cost?

Answer:

QUESTION 6

During the day, a truck driver travels 65.8 km, 36.5 km, 22.7 km and 89.9 km. What is the total distance travelled?

Answer:

QUESTION 7

What is the total length of a trowel with a handle of 15.5 cm and an end of 17.8 cm?

Answer:

QUESTION 8

At a clearance sale, a 3.6-cu ft heavy-duty petrol mixer with adjustable stand costs $2420.50, and a heavy-duty galvanised electric block saw with a 2.2kW motor and 200-mm depth-of-cut costs $3790.50. What is the total cost for both?

Answer:

QUESTION 9

Three invoices are issued for three completed jobs. The first invoice is for $450.80, for the first job. The next invoice is for $1130.65, for the second job and the final invoice is for $660.45, for the last job. What is the total for all three invoices?

Answer:

QUESTION 10

An 18-oz steel hammer with a patented rubber Shock-Blok™ head costs $89.90. How much do four cost?

Answer:

Shutterstock.com/Michal Bellan

Section B: Subtraction

Short-answer questions

Specific instructions to students

- This section is designed to help you to improve your subtraction skills when working with decimals.
- Read the questions below and answer all of them in the spaces provided.
- You may not use a calculator.
- You need to show all working.

QUESTION 1

A bricklayer works on a scaffold platform that is 2.5 metres high. It is lowered by 388 millimetres, then lowered again a further 295 millimetres an hour later.
At what height is the scaffold platform after being lowered for the second time?

Answer:

QUESTION 2

A scaffold platform is lowered by 225 cm from a height of 1.450 m. What is the new height of the scaffold platform?

Answer:

QUESTION 3

An apprentice completes a job and the company charges the client $789.20. The boss then gives the client a discount of $75.50. How much is the final cost?

Answer:

QUESTION 4

An apprentice works 38 hours in a week and earns $345.60. Petrol costs for the week come to $48.85. How much money is left?

Answer:

QUESTION 5

Scaffolding is used to reach the outside area of a house that is 3.60 m high. The scaffolding then needs to be lowered to a height of 2.95 m to work on the next section of the house. How far has the scaffold been lowered?

Answer:

QUESTION 6

Two lengths need to be cut from a 6-m plank. The two lengths measure 2250 mm and 2870 mm. How much is left of the 6-m plank?

Answer:

QUESTION 7

A bricklaying company has an account balance of $4000. If two 3.6-cu ft heavy-duty electric mixer motors are bought for $1550 each, how much money is left in the account?

Answer:

QUESTION 8

A length of timber needs to act as a border for some cement work. The timber measures 1250 mm. If a length of 900 mm is cut from it, how much remains?

Answer:

QUESTION 9

A bricklayer has $5000 in his work account. He purchases a zinc-plated electric brick saw with a 2.3hp motor, a removable stand and large pneumatic wheels for $1850, a 3.5-cu ft heavy-duty petrol mixer motor for $1650, and a mortar saw with 900W motor for toothing out brickwork for $950. How much is left in his account?

Answer:

QUESTION 10

As part of a building project, 2000 blocks are ordered for different jobs. If 350 are used on one job, 765 on another job and 445 on two more jobs, how many blocks are left?

Answer:

Section C: Multiplication

Short-answer questions

Specific instructions to students

- This section is designed to help you to improve your multiplication skills when working with decimals.
- Read the questions below and answer all of them in the spaces provided.
- You may not use a calculator.
- You need to show all working.

QUESTION 1

If a 20-kg bag of mortar costs $19.95, how much do five bags of mortar cost?

Answer:

QUESTION 2

If an apprentice purchases 16 litres of methylated spirits, which cost $3.50 per litre, what is the total cost?

Answer:

QUESTION 3

Six 5-litre containers with measuring cups for mixing mortar are purchased at a cost of $64.50 each. What is the total cost for the six containers?

Answer:

QUESTION 4

Six 8-m fluro green measuring tapes are bought for $8.65 each. What is the total cost?

Answer:

QUESTION 5

An apprentice buys 12 dyna bolts that cost $1.95 each. What is the total cost?

Answer:

QUESTION 6

iStockphoto/lawcain

A scaffolder, who is a contractor for a builder, gets paid $34.50 per hour. If 38 hours are worked in one week, what is the gross wage (before tax)?

Answer:

QUESTION 7

Large stringline holders have been discounted to $2.55 each. If 25 are purchased, how much money has been spent?

Answer:

QUESTION 8

A labourer's car has a 52-litre tank. Fuel costs $1.35 per litre. How much does it cost to fill the tank?

Answer:

QUESTION 9

A bricklayer lays 3400 bricks. Each brick costs $1.10. What is the total cost for the bricks?

Answer:

QUESTION 10

A labourer earns $160.65 per day. What is the gross weekly wage (before tax) for five days of work?

Answer:

Section D: Division

QUESTION 1

An apprentice has 28.5 litres of cleaning fluid that are used on six separate jobs. How much is equally allocated for each job?

Answer:

QUESTION 2

A bricklaying contractor earns $990.50 for five days of work. How much is earned per day?

Answer:

QUESTION 3

A bricklaying company charges $3732.70 to complete some brickwork on a house. It took 50 hours to complete the job, so what is the rate per hour, inclusive of labour and materials?

Answer:

QUESTION 4

A labourer gets paid $600.85 for 27 hours of work. What is the hourly rate?

Answer:

QUESTION 5

A semi-trailer carrying blocks drives from Adelaide to Darwin and completes 3368 km in seven days. On average, what distance has been travelled each day?

Answer:

QUESTION 6

A bricklayer subcontracts an interstate job to one of his mates. The mate needs to drive from Adelaide to Melbourne, travelling a total of 889.95 km to reach the job. The trip takes nine hours of driving time. On average, how far has the mate travelled per hour?

Answer:

QUESTION 7

A work van uses 36 litres to travel 225.8 km. How far does the car travel per litre?

Answer:

QUESTION 8

A bricklayer works for three days and gets paid $840. How much is she paid per day (before tax)?

Answer:

QUESTION 9

A bricklayer charges 0.90 cents per brick that is laid. If $900 is charged, how many bricks have been laid?

Answer:

QUESTION 10

A client is charged a total of $3450 for 3000 bricks laid by a bricklayer. What is the cost to lay each brick?

Answer:

Section A: Addition

QUESTION 1

$\frac{1}{2} + \frac{4}{5} =$

Answer:

_____

QUESTION 2

$2\frac{2}{4} + 1\frac{2}{3} =$

Answer:

_____

QUESTION 3

A labourer puts $\frac{1}{3}$ of a 20-kg cement bag into a mixer. Another $\frac{1}{3}$ of the bag is added. How much of the 20-kg bag has been added to the mixer, as a fraction?

Answer:

_____

QUESTION 4

An apprentice adds $\frac{1}{3}$ of a bag of sand into a mixer. Another $\frac{1}{2}$ of the bag is added. How much sand has been added, as a fraction?

Answer:

_____

QUESTION 5

A bricklayer adds 1 and $\frac{2}{3}$ bags of cement to a mixer. Another 1 and $\frac{1}{4}$ bags is added. What is the total amount of cement added, as a fraction?

Answer:

_____

Section B: Subtraction

QUESTION 1

$\frac{2}{3} - \frac{1}{4} =$

Answer:

_____

QUESTION 2

$2\frac{2}{3} - 1\frac{1}{4} =$

Answer:

_____

QUESTION 3

A labourer has $\frac{2}{3}$ of a brick. He then uses a brick splitter to cut off $\frac{1}{2}$ of the brick. How much is left of the brick, as a fraction?

Answer:

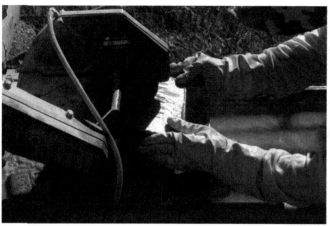

Alamy/jbcn

QUESTION 4

A bag of cement is $\frac{3}{4}$ full. If $\frac{1}{8}$ is used on a job, how much is left, as a fraction?

Answer:

QUESTION 5

There are 2 and $\frac{1}{2}$ bags of sand on site. If 1 and $\frac{1}{3}$ bags are used for a job, how much is left, as a fraction?

Answer:

Section C: Multiplication

Short-answer questions

Specific instructions to students

- This section is designed to help you to improve your multiplication skills when working with fractions.
- Read the questions below and answer all of them in the spaces provided.
- You may not use a calculator.
- You need to show all working.

QUESTION 1

$\frac{2}{4} \times \frac{2}{3} =$

Answer:

QUESTION 2

$2\frac{2}{3} \times 1\frac{1}{2} =$

Answer:

QUESTION 3

iStockphoto/beezeebee

A bricklayer has 15 half bricks. How many full bricks does this make, as a fraction?

Answer:

9780170473880

QUESTION 4

There are 8 and $\frac{1}{2}$ bags of cement on site. If each bag weighs 20 kg, how many kilograms are there in total?

Answer:

QUESTION 5

An apprentice needs 16 half bricks to finish a window. How many full bricks are needed?

Answer:

Section D: Division

Short-answer questions

Specific instructions to students

- This section is designed to help you to improve your division skills when working with fractions.
- Read the questions below and answer all of them in the spaces provided.
- You may not use a calculator.
- You need to show all working.

QUESTION 1

$\frac{2}{3} \div \frac{1}{4} =$

Answer:

QUESTION 2

$2\frac{3}{4} \div 1\frac{1}{3} =$

Answer:

QUESTION 3

A labourer works 37 and $\frac{1}{2}$ hours over five days. How many hours per day has she worked, as a fraction?

Answer:

QUESTION 4

An apprentice works a 40-hour week and spends $\frac{4}{5}$ of the time doing physical labour. How many hours of the working week are spent doing physical labour?

Answer:

QUESTION 5

A labourer moves 20 and a $\frac{1}{2}$ kilograms of cement over three trips. How many kilograms are carried in each trip, as a fraction?

Answer:

Dreamstime/Stanislav Komogorov

Unit 8: Percentages

Short-answer questions

Specific instructions to students

- In this unit, you will be able to practise and improve your skills in working out percentages.
- Read the questions below and answer all of them in the spaces provided.
- You may not use a calculator.
- You need to show all working.

> 10% rule: move the decimal one place to the left to get 10%.

EXAMPLE

10% of $45.00 is $4.50.

QUESTION 1

Brickwork repairs are done for a client, at a cost of $5220.00. The company doing the job gives a discount of 10%.

a How much is the discount worth?

Answer:

b What is the final cost?

Answer:

QUESTION 2

A nail gun costs $249.00. A 10% discount is given at a sale. What is the final cost after 10% is taken off?

Answer:

QUESTION 3

A contractor buys a rotary laser level and detector, complete with staff and tripod, for $698.00. If the contractor is given a 10% discount, how much will the laser level cost?

Answer:

QUESTION 4

A heavy-duty multi-purpose cutter is bought for $24.60. A 5% discount is given.

a How much is the discount worth?

Answer:

b What is the final price? (Hint: Find 10%, halve it and then subtract it from the overall price.)

Answer:

QUESTION 5

A trade's assistant buys three packets of sandpaper for a total of $20, a 14v cordless drill for $69 and two sanding blocks for a total of $10.50.

a How much is the total?

Answer:

b How much is paid after a 10% discount?

Answer:

QUESTION 6

A bricklayer purchases a 3-inch brick bolster with wrist guard for $19.99, a bricklayer's poly-fiber poly-brush for $9.99, a blue clay/concrete premium 230 mm blade for an angle grinder for $89.99, a 150 mm fixed-arm Dutch pin concrete hook for $6.99 and a 15 m extension lead for $14.99.

a What is the total?

Answer:

9780170473880

b What is the final cost after a 10% discount?

Answer:

_____

QUESTION 7

A hardware store offers 20% off the price of 10-mm and 13-mm double-sided jointers. The jointers normally cost $26 each before the discount. How much will they cost after the discount?

Answer:

_____

QUESTION 8

Cordless drills are discounted by 15%. If the regular retail price is $65.00 each, what is the discounted price?

Answer:

_____

QUESTION 9

The regular retail price of a box frame 80A-2/100 level is $56.00. The store has a '20% off' sale. How much will it cost during the sale?

Answer:

_____

QUESTION 10

Shutterstock.com/Martin Christopher Parker

A 13-inch brick trowel with a DuraSoft handle retails for $99. How much does it cost after the store takes off 30% during an end-of-financial-year sale?

Answer:

_____

Unit 9: Measurement Conversions

Short-answer questions

Specific instructions to students

- This unit is designed to help you to improve your skills and to increase your speed in converting one measurement unit into another.
- Read the questions below and answer all of them in the spaces provided.
- You may not use a calculator.
- You need to show all working.

QUESTION 1

How many millimetres are there in 1 cm?

Answer:

QUESTION 2

How many millimetres are there in 1 m?

Answer:

QUESTION 3

How many centimetres are there in 1 m?

Answer:

QUESTION 4

The height of a wall is 2550 mm. What is the height in metres?

Answer:

QUESTION 5

The height of the scaffold platform to be erected measures 3650 mm. How many metres is this?

Answer:

QUESTION 6

The height of the scaffold platform is 2.6 m. How many millimetres is this?

Answer:

QUESTION 7

A scaffold platform is raised in height by 2850 mm. An hour later it is raised a further 3250 mm. What is the total height that the scaffold platform has been raised, in metres?

Answer:

QUESTION 8

A carpenter needs three separate lengths of planks to use on different jobs. The lengths measure 2.45 m, 3.15 m and 1.85 m. What is the total length of the planks, in millimetres?

Answer:

QUESTION 9

The length of a side of a house measures 2580 mm from the front and includes a sill of 325 mm, then continues another 2400 mm to the back of the house. How much does this measure in metres?

Answer:

QUESTION 10

An apprentice is reading from a building plan. He can see that there are four lengths on the plan for the first bedroom. These lengths are 2850 mm, 2350 mm, 2850 mm and 2350 mm. What is the total perimeter of the bedroom, in metres?

Answer:

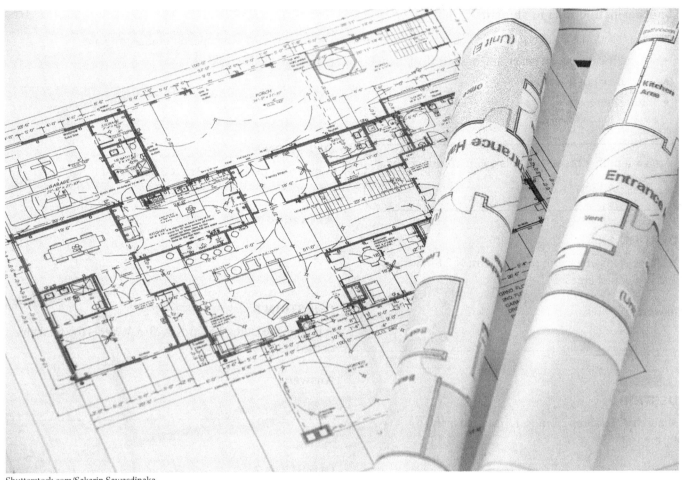

Shutterstock.com/Sakarin Sawasdinaka

Section A: Area

> Area = length × breadth and is given in square units
>
> $= l \times b$

QUESTION 1

The dimensions of a living room are 3 m × 2.8 m wide. What is the total area?

Answer:

QUESTION 2

If a laundry measures 2.2 m × 1.3 m, what is the total area?

Answer:

QUESTION 3

A dining room measures 3.5 m × 3.65 m. What is the total area?

Answer:

QUESTION 4

A toilet area measures 2.1 m × 0.8 m. What is the total area?

Answer:

QUESTION 5

A bedroom measures 3.3 m × 3.5 m. What is the total area?

Answer:

QUESTION 6

A lounge measures 3.55 m × 3.28 m. What is the total area of the lounge?

Answer:

QUESTION 7

The measurement of a carport that will be bricked is 4.5 m × 2.5 m. What is the total area of the carport?

Answer:

QUESTION 8

A kitchen is 3.5 m × 3.2 m. What is the total area?

Answer:

QUESTION 9

A brick shed is 3.2 m wide × 8.6 m long. What is the total area?

Answer:

QUESTION 10

A carport is 2.9 m long × 2.6 m wide. How much floor area is there?

Answer:

iStockphoto/CindyMurray

Section B: Perimeter

Perimeter is the length of all sides added together.

> **Perimeter = length + breadth + length + breadth**

The unit of measurement is either in metres, centimetres or millimetres.

QUESTION 1

Calculate the perimeter of a house that is 13 m long × 9 m wide.

Answer:

QUESTION 2

Work out the perimeter of a room that is 3.2 m × 2.6 m.

Answer:

QUESTION 3

What is the perimeter of a lounge that is 4.8 m × 3.8 m?

Answer:

QUESTION 4

Find the perimeter of a carport that is 6.5 m × 2.7 m.

Answer:

QUESTION 5

What is the perimeter of a bedroom that measures 3.4 m × 3.7 m?

Answer:

QUESTION 6

Work out the perimeter of a kitchen that is 2.85 m × 2.35 m.

Answer:

QUESTION 7

A verandah is 4.65 m × 3.85 m. What is the perimeter?

Answer:

_____

QUESTION 8

A dining room has the dimensions of 3.75 m × 3.95 m. What is the perimeter?

Answer:

_____

QUESTION 9

On a building plan, a garage measures 5.55 m × 4.65 m. What is the perimeter?

Answer:

_____

QUESTION 10

The lounge of an apartment measures 2.75 m × 2.95 m. What is the total perimeter?

Answer:

_____

Section C: Volume of a rectangle

Short-answer questions

Specific instructions to students

- This section is designed to help you to improve your skills and to increase your speed in measuring the volume of a rectangle.
- Read the questions below and answer all of them in the spaces provided.
- You may not use a calculator.
- You need to show all working.

> **Volume = length × width × height and is given in cubic units**
>
> $$= l \times \omega \times h$$

QUESTION 1

An equipment storage shed needs to be built to the dimensions of 13 m × 5 m × 4 m. How many cubic metres is the shed?

Answer:

_____

QUESTION 2

A wall is constructed with the dimensions of 2 m × 1 m × 0.5 m. How many cubic metres is the wall?

Answer:

_____

QUESTION 3

A builder builds a room that measures 4 m long × 3 m high × 3 m wide. How many cubic metres is the room?

Answer:

_____

QUESTION 4

Shutterstock.com/Vadym Andrushchenko

An apprentice bricklayer constructs an interior wall that measures 2.2 m × 1.8 m × 0.5 m. How many cubic metres is the wall?

Answer:

QUESTION 5

A labourer builds a storage area using the dimensions of 60 cm × 15 cm × 50 cm. How many cubic centimetres is the storage area?

Answer:

QUESTION 6

A bathroom shower has the dimensions of 4.2 m × 1.2 m × 1.25 m. What is the cubic area of the shower?

Answer:

QUESTION 7

A tool box is 50 cm long, 30 cm wide and 25 cm tall. How many cubic centimetres are available for storing tools?

Answer:

QUESTION 8

The boot of a work wagon is 1.4 m wide × 1.6 m long × 88 cm high. What is the cubic area of the boot?

Answer:

QUESTION 9

An apprentice works on an internal wall of a shed that is 1.75 m high × 1.35 m wide × 3.6 m long. What is the volume of the wall in cubic metres?

Answer:

QUESTION 10

A builder constructs a wall around a room that measures 3.8 m × 3.8 m × 2.5 m. How many cubic metres is the room?

Answer:

Short-answer questions

Specific instructions to students

- This unit is designed to help you to calculate how much a job is worth and how long you need to complete the job.
- Read the questions below and answer all of them in the spaces provided.
- You may not use a calculator.
- You need to show all working.

QUESTION 1

If a first-year apprentice bricklayer earns $350.40 per week, how much is earned per year? (Remember: there are 52 weeks in a year.)

Answer:

Getty Images/Bart Coenders

QUESTION 2

A labourer starts work at 7.00 a.m. and stops for a break at 9.30 a.m. for 20 minutes. Lunch starts at 1.15 p.m. and is for 30 minutes. The labourer then works until 4 p.m. How many hours have been worked, including breaks?

Answer:

QUESTION 3

A contractor earns $35.00 an hour and works a 38-hour week. How much is his weekly gross earnings (before tax)?

Answer:

QUESTION 4

Over a month, an apprentice working for a small company completes five jobs. After completing the work, he issues invoices for $465.80, $2490.50, $556.20, $1560.70 and $990.60. What is the total to be paid for all of the completed jobs?

Answer:

QUESTION 5

A bricklayer takes 34 minutes to unload materials and tools from the work van. It takes eight minutes to prepare the materials for mixing mortar, four minutes to carry the mortar to the build and 27 minutes to complete the initial bricklaying. How much time has been taken on this job? (Give your answer in hours and minutes.)

Answer:

QUESTION 6

A house is being demolished and it takes the labourer four and a half hours to remove timber and roof sheets. If the company charges a rate of $28.60 an hour, what is the bill for this work?

Answer:

QUESTION 7

An apprentice takes 1.5 hours to complete brickwork on a window. If the apprentice is getting paid $14.80 per hour, what is the total bill?

Answer:

QUESTION 8

A house needs to be repaired after major damage is caused from a car crashing into it. The construction crew spends 116 hours working to repair the house. If they work 8-hour days, how many days does it take to complete the job?

Answer:

Newspix/Jake Nowakowski

QUESTION 9

A work crew begins work at 7.00 a.m. and works until 3.30 p.m. The crew takes a morning break for 20 minutes, a lunch break for 60 minutes and an afternoon break for 20 minutes.

a   How much time has been spent on breaks?

Answer:

b   How much time has been spent working?

Answer:

QUESTION 10

The cost for the bricklayer for a renovation job is $960.00. The bricklayer spent 24 hours on the job. How much is the rate of pay per hour?

Answer:

Section A: Introducing square numbers

Short-answer questions

Specific instructions to students

- This section is designed to help you to improve your skills and to increase your speed in squaring numbers.
- Read the questions below and answer all of them in the spaces provided.
- You may not use a calculator.
- You need to show all working.

Any number squared is multiplied by itself.

EXAMPLE

4 squared $= 4^2 = 4 \times 4 = 16$

QUESTION 1

$6^2 =$

Answer:

QUESTION 2

$8^2 =$

Answer:

QUESTION 3

$12^2 =$

Answer:

QUESTION 4

$3^2 =$

Answer:

QUESTION 5

$7^2 =$

Answer:

QUESTION 6

$11^2 =$

Answer:

QUESTION 7

$10^2 =$

Answer:

QUESTION 8

$9^2 =$

Answer:

QUESTION 9

$2^2 =$

Answer:

QUESTION 10

$4^2 =$

Answer:

Section B: Applying square numbers to the trade

Worded practical problems

Specific instructions to students

- The worded questions make the content relevant to everyday situations.
- Read the questions below and answer all of them in the spaces provided.
- You may not use a calculator.
- You need to show all working.

QUESTION 1

A wet area measures 2.8 m × 2.8 m. What is the total area, in square metres?

Answer:

_____

QUESTION 2

A lounge is 5.2 m × 5.2 m. What is the total area, in square metres?

Answer:

_____

QUESTION 3

The dimensions of a kitchen are 2.6 m × 2.6 m. What is the total area, in square metres?

Answer:

_____

QUESTION 4

An equipment shed needs to be built and needs to measure 15 m × 15 m. An area for storage of small electric tools needs to be built inside the equipment shed and needs to measure 2.4 m × 2.4 m. How much area is left in the equipment shed?

Answer:

_____

QUESTION 5

A house needs to be built with a total floor area of 13.8 m × 13.8 m. One wet area takes up 1.2 m × 1.2 m and another takes up 2.7 m × 2.7 m. How much area is left in the house?

Answer:

_____

QUESTION 6

Shutterstock.com/PlusONE

A bathroom measures 2.4 m × 2.4 m. If 1.65 m × 1.65 m is taken up by the vanity, how much area is left?

Answer:

_____

QUESTION 7

An apprentice is laying bricks for a double wall that is nine bricks across the base and is 29 bricks high. How many bricks are needed for the job?

Answer:

_____

QUESTION 8

A circular flowerbed has a radius of 2 metres and will have a concrete path that is 1 metre wide built around it.

a   Calculate the area of the path, given that $\pi = 3.14$ and Area $= \pi r^2$.

Answer:

_____

b   A concrete company quotes $10 per m². How much will it cost for the concrete path?

Answer:

_____

QUESTION 9

A circular flowerbed has a radius of 2.5 metres and will have a concrete path that is 1 metre wide built around it.

a   Calculate the area of the path, given that $\pi = 3.14$ and Area $= \pi r^2$.

Answer:

_____

b   A concrete company quotes $10 per m². How much will it cost for the concrete path?

Answer:

_____

QUESTION 10

A rectangular flowerbed will have a 1-metre wide concrete path down the two longest sides (6 metres each) and a path down one of its shorter sides (3 metres).
A semi-circular flower bed will join the rectangle where there is no concrete and will have the same 1-metre wide concrete path around it. The radius of the semi-circular path is 1.5 m.

a   Calculate the area of the path, given that $\pi = 3.14$ and Area $= \pi r^2$. (Draw a draft plan of the two areas before attempting to solve this problem.)

Answer:

_____

b   A concrete company quotes $10 per m². How much will it cost for the concrete path for both areas?

Answer:

_____

Shutterstock.com/Vadim Ratnikov

9780170473880

Section A: Introducing ratios

QUESTION 1

A bricklayer uses the ratio of 1 part cement, 3 parts sand and 3 parts aggregate to make concrete for foundation and footings.

a   If 1 part equals 1 kg, how many kilograms of each part are needed?

Answer:

b   How many kilograms in total is the mixture?

Answer:

QUESTION 2

Using the ratio to make concrete from Question 1 (above), how much of each part is needed if 1 part equals 3 kg?

Answer:

QUESTION 3

Using the ratio to make concrete from Question 1, how much of each part is needed if 1 part equals 5 kg?

Answer:

QUESTION 4

Mortar is needed for a bricklaying job. The ratio is 1 part cement and 4 parts sand. If 1 part equals 2 kg, how many kilograms of each part are needed?

Answer:

QUESTION 5

Mortar is needed for a bricklaying job. The ratio is 1 part cement and 4 parts sand. If 1 part equals 4 kg, how many kilograms of each part are needed?

Answer:

QUESTION 6

Mortar is needed for a bricklaying job. The ratio is 1 part cement and 4 parts sand. If 1 part equals 6 kg, how many kilograms of each part are needed?

Answer:

QUESTION 7

Render needs to be made at a ratio of 1 part cement and 3 parts sand. How many kilograms of each part are needed if a total of 16 kg is made up?

Answer:

QUESTION 8

Render needs to be made at a ratio of 1 part cement and 3 parts sand. How many kilograms of each part are needed if a total of 24 kg is made up?

Answer:

_____

QUESTION 9

Render needs to be made at a ratio of 1 part cement and 3 parts sand. How many kilograms of each part are needed if a total of 32 kg is made up?

Answer:

_____

QUESTION 10

Concrete used for a driveway is made at a ratio of 1 part cement, 2 parts sand and 3 parts aggregate. If 24 kg is made up, how many kilograms of each part are needed?

Answer:

_____

Getty Images/small_frog

9780170473880

Section A: The apprentice years

QUESTION 1

A first-year bricklaying apprentice gets paid $12.19 per hour. A travel allowance of $13.07 is also paid per day. If the apprentice works for 31 hours over four days, how much is earned for the working week, including allowances, before tax?

Answer:

QUESTION 2

A first-year bricklaying apprentice gets paid $12.19 per hour. A travel allowance of $13.07 is also paid per day. If the apprentice works for 62 hours over eight days, how much is earned, including allowances, before tax?

Answer:

QUESTION 3

A first-year bricklaying apprentice gets paid $12.19 per hour. A travel allowance of $13.07 is also paid per day. If the apprentice works for 124 hours over 16 days, how much is earned, including allowances, before tax?

Answer:

QUESTION 4

A first-year bricklaying apprentice gets paid $12.19 per hour, with an additional travel allowance of $13.07 per day. The apprentice works for 31 hours over a four-day week. If $50 is spent on petrol, $38 on food and $57 on entertainment, how much is left over?

Answer:

QUESTION 5

A first-year bricklaying apprentice gets paid $12.19 per hour, with an additional travel allowance of $13.07 per day. The apprentice works for 31 hours over a four-day week. If $35.50 is spent on petrol, $47.50 on food and $62.75 on entertainment, how much is left over?

Answer:

QUESTION 6

A second-year bricklaying apprentice gets paid $14.18 per hour, plus $14.82 for a travel allowance per day. The apprentice works for 31 hours over a four-day week. How much is earned, including allowances, before tax?

Answer:

QUESTION 7

A second-year bricklaying apprentice gets paid $14.18 per hour, plus $14.82 for a travel allowance per day. The apprentice works for 62 hours over an eight-day fortnight. How much is earned, including allowances, before tax?

Answer:

QUESTION 8

A second-year bricklaying apprentice gets paid $14.18 per hour, plus $14.82 for a travel allowance per day. The apprentice works for 124 hours over a 16-day month. How much is earned, including allowances, before tax?

Answer:

QUESTION 9

A second-year bricklaying apprentice gets paid $14.18 per hour, plus $14.82 for a travel allowance per day. The apprentice works for 31 hours over four days. If $86 is spent on tools, $49 on PPE gear and $18 on medical insurance, how much is left?

Answer:

_____

QUESTION 10

A second-year bricklaying apprentice gets paid $14.18 per hour, plus $14.82 for a travel allowance per day. The apprentice works for 62 hours over an eight-day fortnight. The apprentice's fortnightly expenses include $45.50 for clothes, $42.90 for food and $180.50 for car registration. How much is left after all the expenses?

Answer:

_____

Section B: Daily bricklaying

Short-answer questions

Specific instructions to students

- This section is designed to help you to improve your Maths skills in the bricklaying trade.
- Read the questions below and answer all of them in the spaces provided.
- You may not use a calculator.
- You need to show all working.
- Reduce the ratios to the simplest or lowest form.

QUESTION 1

Tony is an experienced bricklayer who works 7.75 hours a day in a bricklaying gang. Having a labourer work with the gang (3 : 1) means that they can lay more bricks per day.

a   If Tony lays 500 bricks per day at a rate of 0.90 cents per brick, how much has he earned for the day?

Answer:

_____

b   If Tony works at the same rate for five days, how much will he earn?

Answer:

_____

QUESTION 2

Chris is a bricklayer who works eight hours a day in a bricklaying gang. Having a labourer work with the gang (3 : 1) means that they can lay more bricks per day.

a   If Chris lays 550 bricks per day at a rate of 0.90 cents per brick, how much has he earned for the day?

Answer:

_____

b   If Chris works at the same rate for 12 days over two weeks, how much will he earn?

Answer:

_____

QUESTION 3

Josh is a labourer for a bricklaying gang (3 : 1). He earns $160 per day.

a   How much does Josh earn for a five-day week?

Answer:

_____

b   If Josh spends $18.00 a day on snacks and lunch, how much pay will he have left at the end of the week?

Answer:

_____

9780170473880

QUESTION 4

A bricklaying gang arrives at a worksite expecting a labourer to be working with them. However, the labourer does not turn up for work. The rate that they lay bricks is reduced to 350 for the day. If the rate per brick is $1.05, how much do they earn for the day?

Answer:

QUESTION 5

A bricklaying gang have a productive day and lay 825 bricks. The agreed rate per brick for this job is $1.15.

a How much is earned for the day?

Answer:

b If the gang is able to maintain this rate for six days, how much will they earn?

Answer:

QUESTION 6

A bricklayer, with the help of a labourer, lays 600 bricks a day at a rate of $1.20 per brick.

a What does the bricklayer earn per day?

Answer:

b What does the bricklayer earn for five days?

Answer:

QUESTION 7

Construction on a house is slow and difficult. Only 250 bricks can be laid per day at a rate of $1.15 per brick.

a How much has the bricklayer earned for the day?

Answer:

b If the same working rate continues for three days, how much is earned?

Answer:

QUESTION 8

amana images/Helen King

Over 10 working days, the rate of bricks that are laid by a gang varies. In the first four days, 450 bricks are laid each day. For the next three days, the rate increases to 650 per day, and for the last three days the rate is 550 per day. If the rate per brick is $1.20, how much is earned for the 10 days?

Answer:

QUESTION 9

Over 20 working days, the rate of bricks that are laid by a gang varies for different reasons. In the first five days, 500 bricks are laid each day. For the next five days, the rate increases to 550 per day. Due to poor weather, the rate drops to 250 per day for the next five days. In the last five days, the rate reaches 350 per day. If the rate per brick is $1.15, how much is earned for the 20 days?

Answer:

QUESTION 10

Over 20 working days, the rate of bricks that are laid by a gang varies. For the first five days, a labourer works with the gang and 600 bricks are laid each day. For the next five days, the rate increases to 650 per day. The labourer injures his back and cannot work or be replaced for the following 10 days. The rate drops to 300 per day for the next five days. In the last five days, the rate reaches 350 per day. If the rate per brick is $1.05, how much is earned for the 20 days?

Answer:

Section C: Working rates per hour

QUESTION 1

A bricklayer works seven and a half hours per day for five days. The rate of pay is $26.70 per hour. How much is earned for the week, before tax?

Answer:

QUESTION 2

A bricklayer works seven and a half hours per day for five days. The rate of pay is $35.50 per hour. How much is earned for the week, before tax?

Answer:

QUESTION 3

A bricklayer works seven and a half hours per day for five days. The rate of pay is $42.30 per hour. How much is earned for the week, before tax?

Answer:

QUESTION 4

Due to having to work on Saturdays, a bricklayer works seven and a half hours per day for 12 days. The rate of pay is $26.70 per hour. How much is earned, before tax?

Answer:

QUESTION 5

Urgent work must be completed on a renovation, so a bricklayer works a total of 82 hours over a fortnight to complete the work. The rate of pay is $32.50 per hour. How much is earned for the fortnight, before tax?

Answer:

QUESTION 6

A bricklayer works on a renovation for a fortnight. He works for seven and a half hours per day for five days a week, over two weeks. He also works on two Saturdays for five more hours each. The rate of pay averages out at $36.30 per hour. How much is earned for the fortnight, including the Saturdays, before tax?

Answer:

iStockphoto/Sergei Butorin

QUESTION 7

A bricklayer works 20 days over a month. He works for seven and a half hours per day. The rate of pay is $32.50 per hour. How much is earned for the month, before tax?

Answer:

QUESTION 8

A highly skilled and experienced bricklayer works 20 days over a month. He works for seven and a half hours per day. The rate of pay is $42.50 per hour. How much is earned for the month, before tax?

Answer:

QUESTION 9

A skilled and experienced bricklayer works 40 days over two months. He works for eight hours per day. The rate of pay is $39.80 per hour. How much is earned for the two months, before tax?

Answer:

QUESTION 10

A highly skilled and experienced bricklayer works 60 days over three months. He works for seven and a half hours per day. The rate of pay is $36.50 per hour. How much is earned for the three months, before tax?

Answer:

Section D: Brickwork and concrete

Short-answer questions

Specific instructions to students

- This section is designed to help you to improve your Maths skills in the bricklaying trade.
- Read the questions below and answer all of them in the spaces provided.
- You may not use a calculator.
- You need to show all working.
- Reduce the ratios to the simplest or lowest form.

QUESTION 1

A bricklayer plans to build a wall and estimates that there are 50 bricks to each square metre. How many bricks are needed for a 7 m × 1 m wall?

Answer:

QUESTION 2

A bricklayer plans to build a wall and estimates that there are 50 bricks to each square metre. How many bricks are needed for a 6 m × 2 m wall?

Answer:

QUESTION 3

A bricklayer plans to build two identical walls and estimates that there are 55 bricks to each square metre. Each wall measures 8 m long and 1 m high. How many bricks are needed?

Answer:

QUESTION 4

A bricklayer plans to build three different walls and estimates that there are 55 bricks to each square metre. The dimensions of the three walls are 5 m × 1 m, 6 m × 1 m and 8 m × 2 m. How many bricks are needed, in total?

Answer:

QUESTION 5

A bricklayer plans to build two walls and estimates that there are 50 bricks to each square metre. The dimensions for the two walls are 3000 mm × 2000 mm and 4000 mm × 1000 mm. How many bricks are needed for both walls?

Answer:

QUESTION 6

A bricklayer refers to building plans and sees that two walls need to be built. The walls measure 3500 mm × 1000 mm and 4500 mm × 1000 mm, respectively. He estimates that there are 50 bricks to each square metre.

a   How many bricks are needed for the two walls?

Answer:

b   If the bricklayer gets paid $1.05 per brick, how much will he earn?

Answer:

QUESTION 7

A bricklayer refers to building plans and sees that two walls need to be built. The walls measure 4500 mm × 1500 mm and 5500 mm × 1500 mm, respectively. She estimates that there are 50 bricks to each square metre.

a   How many bricks are needed for the two walls?

Answer:

b   If the bricklayer gets paid $0.90 per brick, how much will she earn?

Answer:

QUESTION 8

A bricklayer needs to build a double brick wall that measures 24 bricks along the base and is 32 bricks high.

a   How many bricks are needed to build the wall?

Answer:

b   What is the final cost for the bricks, if each brick is $1.15?

Answer:

QUESTION 9

Three double brick walls need to be constructed. Each brick wall measures eight bricks along the base and is 34 bricks high.

a   How many bricks are needed to build the walls?

Answer:

b   What is the final cost for the bricks, if each brick is $1.10?

Answer:

QUESTION 10

A wall contains 3084 bricks, which were laid at a cost of $1.20 per brick. What is the total cost for the bricks?

Answer:

Bricklaying
Practice Written Exam for the Bricklaying Trade

Reading time: 10 minutes

Writing time: 1 hour 30 minutes

Section A: Literacy

Section B: General Mathematics

Section C: Trade Mathematics

QUESTION and ANSWER BOOK

Section	Topic	Number of questions	Marks
A	Literacy	7	22
B	General Mathematics	11	26
C	Trade Mathematics	44	52
		Total 62	Total 100

The sections may be completed in the order of your choice.

NO CALCULATORS are to be used during the exam.

Spelling

Read the passage below and then underline the 20 spelling errors.

10 marks

Two prospactive bricklayers, Zach and Tom, wanted to know about the bricklaying trade. They asked around some construction sites and they found that there is a general concensus held by many in the building industry that brick cleaning is a problem. Bad brick cleanning can damage good brickwork deseign, good brick selection and laying. Zach and Tom were told that, in the past, bricklayers often cleaned their own work. But more recently, brick cleaning is considared to be a separate trade. They were also told that good bricklayers will keep brickwork clean while laying, and will leave minimum moretar on the 'face'. There is always some cleaning down required, mainly to get rid of mortar droppings or any other stains that can accummulate or build up during the building process.

Zach and Tom were surprised to hear that brick cleaning has devaloped into a seperate trade and that the head contractor often becomes more concerned than the bricklayer about mortar staining.

Some arckitects are fammiliar with the damage caused to brick faces and are worried about poor joints and damage to other elements from excesive cleaning, due to high pressure apliances.

One of the workers that Zach and Tom spoke to suggested that a solution is to make the brick cleaning trade more uniform by training and lisensing people, or another option is to elimminate the trade and revert the responsibility of cleaning back to bricklayers.

'What about mortar?' asked Zach. 'What about it?' said Tom. 'Well, what is it made of?' asked Zach. After some research, the boys found that much brickwork is laid in 1 : 1 : 6 cement, lyme and sand mortar. A large colour range is possible if the mix uses the ratio of 1 : 1 : 6. To whitan up mortar, white cemant is added, but this is rare mainly due to cost. Several ready-mix mortars use whitar sands than most bricklayers' site-mixed mortars, which are between 50 per cent and 75 per cent bush sand. Some mixes have a yellow ochre colour added by increasing the bush sand contant.

Correct the spelling errors by writing them out with the correct spelling below.

_____

_____

Alphabetising

Put the following words into alphabetical order.

7 marks

Point	Safety googles
Chalk line	Lime
Aggregate	Safety boots
Waterproofing	Gloves
Mortar	Blocks
Corner block	Scaffold
Pier	Mixer

_____

_____

_____

_____

_____

_____

_____

_____

_____

_____

_____

_____

_____

_____

Comprehension

Short-answer questions

Specific instructions to students

- Read the following passage and answer the questions using full sentences.

The trainers at a registered training organisation (RTO) explain to the apprentices that bricklaying in extreme weather conditions requires certain considerations to make sure that the job is successful. Different weather conditions, such as hot and cold climates, can affect the bricklaying process, so it is important to know how to work to suit the weather. If bricks are not laid in the correct way, appropriate to the weather conditions, it could lead to inferior brickwork, which may be dangerous.

Different bricklaying procedures are required for hot and cold weather. The weather can affect the mortar, which is the material that holds the bricks together. The mortar's ability to set in varied weather conditions can be compromised if the bricklayer does not take the appropriate steps to check it.

Hot weather can affect the way that bricks set, particularly in countries prone to heat, such as Australia, South Africa and India. It is easier to lay bricks in hot weather if adequate water is available. When laying bricks in the heat, a bricklayer should consider that bricks with a high-absorption rate will easily soak up a lot of moisture from the mortar. This causes a reduction to the quality of the adhesion and strength of the wall. The bricks may need to be dampened to reduce the chance of this happening. It is important not to dampen low-absorption bricks as this may create excessive fluid, resulting in an unstable wall.

Mortar is a mixture of sand, water and a binder, which could be cement or lime. In hot weather, mortar with a high lime content is recommended and preferred by many bricklayers. It is also a good idea to keep mortar in a shaded area, if possible. Another recommendation is to use cool water to mix mortar and grout and keep mortar and grout at temperatures below 49°C. It needs to be used within two hours of mixing. Be sure to keep all equipment that makes contact with the mortar in a shaded area. Also, it is a recommended to pour cool water over mixers and mortar boards before they come into contact with mortar.

QUESTION 1   1 mark

What are the different weather conditions that can affect the bricklaying process?

Answer:

_____

_____

QUESTION 2   1 mark

Why do bricks need to be laid in the 'correct way', appropriate to the weather conditions? What can happen as an outcome if they are not laid correctly?

Answer:

_____

_____

QUESTION 3   1 mark

What material can be affected by the weather, which can cause poor brickwork?

Answer:

_____

_____

QUESTION 4   1 mark

Which countries are prone to hot weather affecting brickwork?

Answer:

_____

_____

QUESTION 5   1 mark

What is used in a mortar mix?

Answer:

_____

_____

Section B: General Mathematics

QUESTION 1   1+1+1 = 3 marks

What unit of measurement would you use to measure:

a   the length of a wall on a building plan?

Answer:

_____

b   the height of a scaffold platform?

Answer:

_____

c   the amount of mortar mixed?

Answer:

_____

QUESTION 2   1+1+1 = 3 marks

Give examples of how the following might be used in the bricklaying trade.

a   Percentage

Answer:

_____

b   Decimals

Answer:

_____

c   Fractions

Answer:

_____

QUESTION 3   1+1 = 2 marks

Convert the following units.

a   1 kg to grams

Answer:

_____

b   1500 g to kilograms

Answer:

_____

QUESTION 4   2 marks

Write the following in descending order.

0.7   0.71   7.1   70.1   701.00   7.0

Answer:

_____

QUESTION 5   1+1 = 2 marks

Write the decimal number that is between:

a   0.1 and 0.2

Answer:

_____

b   1.3 and 1.4

Answer:

_____

QUESTION 6   1+1 = 2 marks

Round off the following numbers to two (2) decimal places.

a   5.177

Answer:

_____

b   12.655

Answer:

_____

QUESTION 7   1+1 = 2 marks

Estimate the following by approximation.

a 101×81

Answer:

_____

b 399×21

Answer:

_____

QUESTION 8   1+1 = 2 marks

What do the following add up to?

a $25, $13.50 and $165.50

Answer:

_____

b $4, $5.99 and $229.50

Answer:

_____

QUESTION 9   1+1 = 2 marks

Subtract the following.

a   196 from 813

Answer:

_____

b   5556 from 9223

Answer:

_____

QUESTION 10   1+1 = 2 marks

Use division to solve the following.

a $4824 \div 3 =$

Answer:

_____

b $84.2 \div 0.4 =$

Answer:

_____

QUESTION 11 $2+2 = 4$ marks

Using BODMAS, solve the following.

a $(3 \times 7) \times 4 + 9 - 5 =$

Answer:

b $(8 \times 12) \times 2 + 8 - 4 =$

Answer:

Section C: Trade Mathematics

Basic Operations

Addition

QUESTION 1   1 mark

A bricklayer purchases 36 bags of cement, 144 concrete blocks and 15 bags of cable ties. How many items have been purchased in total?

Answer:

QUESTION 2   1 mark

Three specialist bricklaying tools are purchased for $25, $45 and $17. What is the total cost?

Answer:

Subtraction

QUESTION 1   1 mark

A bricklayer uses 57 cable ties from a box that contains 150 cable ties. How many remain?

Answer:

QUESTION 2   1 mark

An apprentice purchases personal protective equipment (PPE) and the total comes to $124. The manager of the shop takes off a discount of $35 during a sale. How much does the apprentice pay?

Answer:

Multiplication

QUESTION 1   1 mark

A bricklayer lays 350 bricks at $1.15 per brick. What is the total cost to the client?

Answer:

QUESTION 2   1 mark

An apprentice bricklayer lays 160 bricks in the first week, 200 bricks in the second week and 250 bricks in the third week. Each brick is laid at 0.90 cents per brick. What is the total cost to the client?

Answer:

Division

QUESTION 1   1 mark

An invoice for a bricklaying job comes to $5578, which is the cost for completing renovations on a house. If the work took six days to complete, what is the average cost per day?

Answer:

QUESTION 2   1 mark

At a yearly stocktake, a store-person counts 72 bags of 20-kg cement. If 12 bags are packed onto each pallet, how many pallets are there?

Answer:

Decimals

Addition

QUESTION 1   1 mark

A labourer buys a bricklayer's poly-fibre brush for $11.95, a 150 mm concrete hook fixed arm for $9.50 and a 25-mm top clamp (L bracket only) for $24.50. How much is charged for the purchase?

Answer:

QUESTION 2   1 mark

During a Christmas sale, a store sells a 20-mm top clamp (nail bracket only) for $7.95, a 10-mm roll jointer for $11.50 and a grooved plugging chisel for $12.85. What is the total for all three items?

Answer:

Subtraction

QUESTION 1   1 mark

A casual labourer earns $418.50 for two days of work. He spends $35.95 on clothes and $25.50 on food? How much money does he have left?

Answer:

QUESTION 2   1 mark

A manager purchases a blue steel wheelbarrow for $124.50. If she pays for it with three $50 notes, how much change is given?

Answer:

Multiplication

QUESTION 1   1 mark

An apprentice buys three metal body rakers with poly wheels, valued at $12.95 each.

a How much does it cost for the three rakers?

Answer:

b How much change is given from $50.00?

Answer:

QUESTION 2   1 mark

Four post hole shovels with long fiberglass handles are purchased at a cost of $28.50 each.

a What is the total cost?

Answer:

b How much change is given from $120.00?

Answer:

Division

QUESTION 1   1 mark

The bricklayer earns $987.00 for five days of work.
How much is earned per day?

Answer:

_____

QUESTION 2   1 mark

Four extra heavy-duty brick carriers cost $88.80. What
is the cost of each?

Answer:

_____

Fractions

QUESTION 1   1 mark

$\frac{1}{4} + \frac{1}{2} =$

Answer:

_____

QUESTION 2   1 mark

$\frac{4}{5} - \frac{1}{3} =$

Answer:

_____

QUESTION 3   1 mark

$\frac{2}{3} \times \frac{1}{4} =$

Answer:

_____

QUESTION 4   1 mark

$\frac{3}{4} \div \frac{1}{2} =$

Answer:

_____

Percentages

QUESTION 1   1 mark

A tool company has a '10% off' sale on all items.
A customer purchases items for $149.00. What is the
final sale price after the discount has been given?

Answer:

_____

QUESTION 2   1 mark

Bricklaying products are discounted by 20% in a
store. If the regular retail price of the products being
purchased comes to $120.00, how much does the
customer pay after the discount?

Answer:

_____

Measurement Conversions

QUESTION 1   1 mark

How many grams are in 1.85 kg?

Answer:

_____

QUESTION 2   1 mark

How many centimetres are in 35 mm?

Answer:

_____

Measurement – Area, Perimeter and Volume

Area

QUESTION 1   1 mark

The floor area of a warehouse measures 15 m × 6 m.
What is the total floor area?

Answer:

_____

QUESTION 2   1 mark

What is the total area of a window that measures 2.2 m × 1.5 m?

Answer:

_____

Perimeter

QUESTION 1   1 mark

Calculate the perimeter of a path that is 13 m long × 3 m wide.

Answer:

_____

QUESTION 2   1 mark

What is the perimeter of a bedroom that measures 2.4 m × 2.7 m?

Answer:

_____

Volume of a rectangle

QUESTION 1   1 mark

An equipment storage shed needs to be built with the dimensions of 12 m × 4 m × 4 m. How many cubic metres is the shed?

Answer:

_____

QUESTION 2   1 mark

A shower has the following dimensions: 1.2 m × 1.2 m × 2.2 m. What is the cubic area of the shower?

Answer:

_____

Earning Wages

QUESTION 1   1 mark

A first-year apprentice bricklayer gets paid $12.50 per hour. If he works for 31 hours over four days, how much is his gross pay?

Answer:

_____

QUESTION 2   1 mark

An apprentice spends the following amount of time on tasks: 17 minutes, 35 minutes, 19 minutes, 48 minutes and 58 minutes.

a   How many minutes were used to complete the tasks?

Answer:

_____

b   How much time was taken in hours and minutes?

Answer:

_____

Squaring Numbers

QUESTION 1   1 mark

What is 7^2?

Answer:

_____

QUESTION 2   1 mark

A garage floor area measures 13 m × 13 m. What is the total floor area?

Answer:

_____

Ratios

QUESTION 1   2 marks

To make up concrete, a bricklayer uses the ratio of
1 part cement, 3 parts sand and 3 parts aggregate.

a   If 1 part equals 3 kg, how many kilograms of each
part are needed?

Answer:

_____

b   How many kilograms in total is the mixture?

Answer:

_____

QUESTION 2   2 marks

To make up concrete for foundation and footings, a
bricklayer uses the ratio of 1 part cement, 3 parts sand
and 3 parts aggregate.

a   If 1 part equals 5 kg, how many kilograms of each
part are needed?

Answer:

_____

b   How many kilograms in total is the mixture?

Answer:

_____

Applying Maths to the Bricklaying Trade

The apprentice years

QUESTION 1   2 marks

A first-year bricklaying apprentice gets paid $12.19 per
hour. A travel allowance of $13.07 is also paid per day.
If the apprentice works for 31 hours over four days,
how much is earned for the working week, including
allowances, before tax?

Answer:

_____

QUESTION 2   2 marks

A first-year bricklaying apprentice gets paid $12.19
per hour. A travel allowance of $13.07 is also paid per
day. If the apprentice works for 62 hours over an eight-
day fortnight, how much is earned for the working
fortnight, including allowances, before tax?

Answer:

_____

Daily bricklaying

QUESTION 1   2 marks

Romeo is an experienced bricklayer who works 7.5
hours a day in a bricklaying gang. Having a labourer
work with the gang (3 : 1) means that they can lay more
bricks per day.

a   If Romeo lays 450 bricks per day at a rate of
0.90 cents per brick, how much has he earned for
the day?

Answer:

_____

b   If Romeo works at the same rate for five days, how
much will he earn?

Answer:

_____

QUESTION 2   2 marks

Phil is an experienced bricklayer who works eight
hours a day in a bricklaying gang (3 : 1). Having a
labourer work with the gang (3 : 1) means that they
can lay more bricks per day.

a   If Phil lays 550 bricks per day at a rate of $1.15 per
brick, how much has he earned for the day?

Answer:

_____

b   If Phil works at the same rate for five days, how
much will he earn?

Answer:

_____

Working rates per hour

QUESTION 1   1 mark

A bricklayer works seven and a half hours per day for five days. The rate of pay is $29.70 per hour. How much is earned for the week, before tax?

Answer:

_____

QUESTION 2   1 mark

A bricklayer works seven and a half hours per day for six days. The rate of pay is $32.90 per hour. How much is earned for the week, before tax?

Answer:

_____

Brickwork and concrete

QUESTION 1   2 marks

A bricklayer plans to build a wall and estimates that there are 55 bricks to each square metre. How many bricks are needed for a six metre wall?

Answer:

_____

QUESTION 2   2 marks

A bricklayer refers to building plans and sees that two walls need to be built. The walls measure 4500 mm × 1000 mm and 5500 mm × 1000 mm, respectively. He estimates that there are 55 bricks to each square metre.

a   How many bricks are needed for the two walls?

Answer:

_____

b   If the bricklayer gets paid $1.05 per brick, how much will he earn?

Answer:

_____

Glossary

Aggregate   A mixture of sand, pebbles or gravel, which is combined with a cement agent to make concrete.

Cavity wall   A hollow wall, generally consisting of two brick walls erected 40 to 50 mm apart, often joined together with ties of metal.

Cement   A mixture of crushed clay and limestone used for making mortar or concrete.

Control joint   A joint or space built into a structure, which allows for expansion, shrinkage and movement due to temperature variations.

Corner block   A concrete masonry unit that has a flat end, used for ending a wall or constructing a corner.

Damp-proofing   The process of coating the outside of a block, concrete or wood foundation wall with a special material to stop moisture from surrounding soil getting in.

Expansion joint   A joint built into a concrete or masonry structure, which allows for expansion without causing any structural damage.

Face   The uncovered surface of a wall or masonry unit.

Footing   Enlargement at the base of a column or foundation wall.

Foundation wall   The supporting structure found below grade. It is comprised of the footing with the foundation wall.

Lime   The principal material used in mortar. Lime makes the mortar more workable and gives it a degree of flexibility, which prevents cracks due to wall movement.

Masonry   Mortar bonds with materials to form a wall.

Mortar   A mixture of lime, cement, sand and water, used to bond bricks, stones or blocks together.

Pier   A column of masonry in isolation.

Point   The process of pushing mortar into the space between laid bricks. Usually done with a pointing trowel.

Reinforced concrete   Concrete that has steel bars, reinforcement wire or wire mesh embedded into it. Usually used for slabs and beams requiring extra strength.

Tie   A strip of metal inserted into the mortar joint, which attaches the masonry units to the wall behind.

Waterproofing   The process of coating the outside of a block, concrete or brick wall with a special material to keep out both liquid water and moisture.

Formulae and Data

Area

Area $= l \times b$
Area = length × breadth and is given in square units

Perimeter

Perimeter is the length of all sides added together.
Perimeter = length + breadth + length + breadth
Volume $= l + b + l + b$

Volume of a rectangle

Volume = length × width × height and is given in cubic units
Volume $= l \times w \times h$

Times Tables

1

1 × 1	=	1
2 × 1	=	2
3 × 1	=	3
4 × 1	=	4
5 × 1	=	5
6 × 1	=	6
7 × 1	=	7
8 × 1	=	8
9 × 1	=	9
10 × 1	=	10
11 × 1	=	11
12 × 1	=	12

2

1 × 2	=	2
2 × 2	=	4
3 × 2	=	6
4 × 2	=	8
5 × 2	=	10
6 × 2	=	12
7 × 2	=	14
8 × 2	=	16
9 × 2	=	18
10 × 2	=	20
11 × 2	=	22
12 × 2	=	24

3

1 × 3	=	3
2 × 3	=	6
3 × 3	=	9
4 × 3	=	12
5 × 3	=	15
6 × 3	=	18
7 × 3	=	21
8 × 3	=	24
9 × 3	=	27
10 × 3	=	30
11 × 3	=	33
12 × 3	=	36

4

1 × 4	=	4
2 × 4	=	8
3 × 4	=	12
4 × 4	=	16
5 × 4	=	20
6 × 4	=	24
7 × 4	=	28
8 × 4	=	32
9 × 4	=	36
10 × 4	=	40
11 × 4	=	44
12 × 4	=	48

5

1 × 5	=	5
2 × 5	=	10
3 × 5	=	15
4 × 5	=	20
5 × 5	=	25
6 × 5	=	30
7 × 5	=	35
8 × 5	=	40
9 × 5	=	45
10 × 5	=	50
11 × 5	=	55
12 × 5	=	60

6

1 × 6	=	6
2 × 6	=	12
3 × 6	=	18
4 × 6	=	24
5 × 6	=	30
6 × 6	=	36
7 × 6	=	42
8 × 6	=	48
9 × 6	=	54
10 × 6	=	60
11 × 6	=	66
12 × 6	=	72

7

1 × 7	=	7
2 × 7	=	14
3 × 7	=	21
4 × 7	=	28
5 × 7	=	35
6 × 7	=	42
7 × 7	=	49
8 × 7	=	56
9 × 7	=	63
10 × 7	=	70
11 × 7	=	77
12 × 7	=	84

8

1 × 8	=	8
2 × 8	=	16
3 × 8	=	24
4 × 8	=	32
5 × 8	=	40
6 × 8	=	48
7 × 8	=	56
8 × 8	=	64
9 × 8	=	72
10 × 8	=	80
11 × 8	=	88
12 × 8	=	96

9

1 × 9	=	9
2 × 9	=	18
3 × 9	=	27
4 × 9	=	36
5 × 9	=	45
6 × 9	=	54
7 × 9	=	63
8 × 9	=	72
9 × 9	=	81
10 × 9	=	90
11 × 9	=	99
12 × 9	=	108

10

1 × 10	=	10
2 × 10	=	20
3 × 10	=	30
4 × 10	=	40
5 × 10	=	50
6 × 10	=	60
7 × 10	=	70
8 × 10	=	80
9 × 10	=	90
10 × 10	=	100
11 × 10	=	110
12 × 10	=	120

11

1 × 11	=	11
2 × 11	=	22
3 × 11	=	33
4 × 11	=	44
5 × 11	=	55
6 × 11	=	66
7 × 11	=	77
8 × 11	=	88
9 × 11	=	99
10 × 11	=	110
11 × 11	=	121
12 × 11	=	132

12

1 × 12	=	12
2 × 12	=	24
3 × 12	=	36
4 × 12	=	48
5 × 12	=	60
6 × 12	=	72
7 × 12	=	84
8 × 12	=	96
9 × 12	=	108
10 × 12	=	120
11 × 12	=	132
12 × 12	=	144

Multiplication Grid

	1	2	3	4	5	6	7	8	9	10	11	12
1	1	2	3	4	5	6	7	8	9	10	11	12
2	2	4	6	8	10	12	14	16	18	20	22	24
3	3	6	9	12	15	18	21	24	27	30	33	36
4	4	8	12	16	20	24	28	32	36	40	44	48
5	5	10	15	20	25	30	35	40	45	50	55	60
6	6	12	18	24	30	36	42	48	54	60	66	72
7	7	14	21	28	35	42	49	56	63	70	77	84
8	8	16	24	32	40	48	56	64	72	80	88	96
9	9	18	27	36	45	54	63	72	81	90	99	108
10	10	20	30	40	50	60	70	80	90	100	110	120
11	11	22	33	44	55	66	77	88	99	110	121	132
12	12	24	36	48	60	72	84	96	108	120	132	144

Notes

Notes

9780170473880

Notes

Notes

Notes

Notes

9780170473880

Notes

Notes